A modern equinoctial mean-time sundial, the Dolphin Dial at the National Maritime Museum, Greenwich. The dial plate is engraved with hour lines that conform to the equation of time correction curves, such that the gap between the shadows of the dolphin's tails, passing over these lines, indicates clock time, either Greenwich Mean Time (GMT) or British Summer Time (BST), to within a minute. The dial was designed by the author in 1977, to celebrate the Silver Jubilee of Queen Elizabeth II, and was executed by Edwin Russell, a leading British sculptor, of Brookbrae Ltd of London.

Sundials

Christopher St J. H. Daniel

A Shire book

Published in 2004 by Shire Publications Ltd,
Cromwell House, Church Street, Princes Risborough,
Buckinghamshire HP27 9AA, UK.
(Website: www.shirebooks.co.uk)

Copyright © 1986 and 2004 by
Christopher St J. H. Daniel.
First published 1986; reprinted 1990, 1993, 1997 and 2000.
Second edition, revised and illustrated in colour, 2004.
Shire Album 176. ISBN 0 7478 0558 X.
Christopher St J. H. Daniel is hereby identified as the
author of this work in accordance with Section 77 of the
Copyright, Designs and Patents Act 1988.

British Library Cataloguing in Publication Data:
Daniel, Christopher St J. H.
Sundials. – 2nd ed. – (Shire album; 176)
1. Sundials
I. Title
681.1'112
ISBN 0 7478 0558 X

Cover: *One of the finest multiple sundials in Britain, probably dating from the reign of Charles II in the late seventeenth century, is in the gardens of Moccas Court in Herefordshire. On the south face it bears the legend 'Philippus Jones fecit', carved by the stonemason who made the dial. In its original state the sundial might well have been a startling sight to modern eyes, probably painted white, delineated in red, blue, green and black, and embellished with gold. Remarkably, there are still traces of some of these lines, as well as the remains of the iron gnomons. Of the thirty-one component dials, most of which are scaphe dials, only the larger ones served a useful purpose, the remainder being primarily symbolic.*

ACKNOWLEDGEMENTS
The author wishes to thank friends and colleagues for their help in the preparation of this book, in particular Richard Riddick and David Cutts of the DPC, and Othens at Linear House, Greenwich. Photographs are acknowledged as follows: Peter Corley, page 43 (upper left); Corpus Christi College, Oxford, page 31 (top right); Gosport Town Council, page 53 (upper right); Andrew Grice Photography / DPC, page 53 (centre left); Hi-Cam Ltd, page 42 (upper left); Cadbury Lamb, pages 27 (centre right), 35 (upper left and lower right), 54; Sir Mark Lennox-Boyd, page 53 (lower right); Longwood Gardens, USA, page 42 (centre left); National Maritime Museum, Greenwich, page 39 (top right); Oglander Roman Trust, page 6 (lower left); Charles Pommier, *L'Astronomie*, page 47 (lower right); QINETIQ (D. A. Bateman), page 23 (upper left); Suzanne Ross, page 4; Royal Greenwich Observatory, page 51 (centre left); Robert Sylvester, page 7 (upper right); G. P. Woodford, page 45 (centre right); York Glaziers' Trust, page 26 (upper left).
The author also wishes to thank all those persons or bodies who allowed him to take photographs on their premises, in particular Green College, Oxford; the Marine Society; the Merchant Adventurers' Company, York; the owners of Moccas Court (front cover); the National Maritime Museum; the National Memorial Arboretum; the National Trust (Buckland Abbey); Queens' College, Cambridge; Peter Tompkins, Cambridge; HM Tower of London; and the UK Hydrographic Office at Taunton.

Printed in Malta by Gutenberg Press Limited, Gudja Road, Tarxien PLA 19, Malta.

Contents

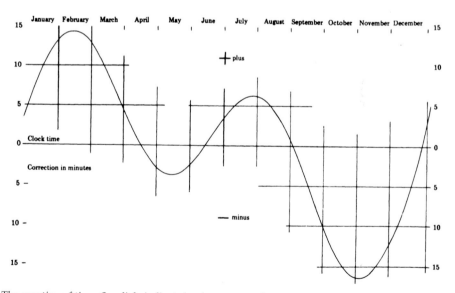

The equation of time. Sundials indicate local apparent solar time. To obtain local mean solar time, follow the correction curve until it coincides with the date on the horizontal scale. Read off the correction in minutes on the vertical scale, designated plus or minus. Apply this correction to the time shown by the sundial. To obtain Greenwich Mean Time, allow a correction for the longitude of the sundial at the rate of four minutes for every one degree of longitude, plus for longitude west, minus for longitude east. When British Summer Time is in force add one hour.

A seventeenth-century common or garden horizontal sundial, which has been taken and used as a keyhole plate for the local church at Sydenham, Oxfordshire. (It does not work as a vertical dial.)

Introduction

Sundial hunting does not require much effort, but it is an addictive pursuit. The purpose of this book is to help people to know what to look for and to understand what they are looking at when they find it.

Sundials fall into two main categories, namely *fixed* sundials and *portable* sundials. Fixed sundials are those which are normally found outside, attached to a building, fixed to a pillar, or on a pedestal in a garden. Portable sundials, though nowadays usually kept indoors, used to be carried around by gentlemen of leisure before the days of pocket watches. Such dials are now mostly collectors' pieces and some can be seen in museums. This book is concerned only with fixed sundials.

A sundial is an instrument which determines the time from the sun by using an indicator, called a *gnomon* or *style*, to cast a shadow or to project a spot of light on to a graduated surface. The time obtained (sundial time) is termed *apparent solar time*. It differs from clock time by an amount known as the *equation of time*, caused partly by the varying speed at which the earth travels in its path round the sun, and partly by the fact that the axis of the earth is tilted some $23^{1}/_{2}$ degrees to the plane of its orbit. Clock time is a convenient but entirely artificial *mean time* of these variations and for national if not commercial reasons is normally based upon a standard time zone, such as Greenwich, whence the term *Greenwich Mean Time* (GMT). However, when

The Signs of the Zodiac

Season	Symbol	Latin name	English name	Date of Sun's entrance
SPRING SIGNS	♈	Aries	The Ram	March 21
	♉	Taurus	The Bull	April 20
	♊	Gemini	The Twins	May 21
SUMMER SIGNS	♋	Cancer	The Crab	June 21
	♌	Leo	The Lion	July 23
	♍	Virgo	The Virgin	August 23
AUTUMN SIGNS	♎	Libra	The Balance	September 23
	♏	Scorpius	The Scorpion	October 24
	♐	Sagittarius	The Archer	November 22
WINTER SIGNS	♑	Capricornus	The Goat	December 22
	♒	Aquarius	The Water-Bearer	January 20
	♓	Pisces	The Fishes	February 19

applying the equation of time correction to a sundial reading to obtain clock time, the actual mean time obtained will be *local mean time*, to which the difference in the longitude between the meridian on which the sundial is situated and the meridian on which the standard time zone is based must be applied to obtain *standard time*, which in Britain is GMT.

Depending on their construction, sundials determine the time by measuring the height of the sun (*altitude*) or by measuring the direction of the sun (bearing or *azimuth*) on a given date, or by a combination of both these factors. Accordingly, a sundial may be described as an altitude dial or as an azimuth dial, and all dials, other than altitude dials, are *directional* in the sense that they must be accurately aligned in order to function correctly.

Fixed sundials have been divided into two classes: primary dials and secondary dials. *Primary* dials are those drawn on the plane of the horizon, called *horizontal* dials, or those drawn perpendicular to it, on the planes either of the prime vertical (to face directly north or south) or the meridian (to face directly east or west), called *vertical* dials. To these are also usually added those drawn on the equinoctial and polar planes. Of these, the *equinoctial* sundial is the fundamental dial in the whole science of gnomonics, from which all other dials may be derived. *Secondary* dials are all those which are drawn on the planes of other circles, besides the horizon, prime vertical, meridian, equinoctial and polar circles, namely those circles which either decline, incline, procline, recline or deincline.

Fixed sundials are traditionally adorned with a motto or saying, often with a reference to the passage of time. Such mottoes have been gathered together and published from time to time and may be found in various reference works.

One of the earliest so-called 'scientific' sundials, probably dating from the late fifteenth or early sixteenth century, showing the equal-hours system, which we use today. The dial is cut into the south wall of Litlington church in East Sussex. The gnomon is missing but would probably have been a triangular piece of metal, jutting out at right angles to the wall. The sloping edge of the plate would have been aligned with the earth's axis, pointing to the north celestial pole, and its shadow would have indicated the time.

History and development

The origin of the sundial is lost in antiquity, but the relationship between time and his own shadow would not have gone unnoticed by primitive man. So perhaps man himself was the first sundial. Likewise the direction and length of the shadows of different objects, trees, rocks or buildings would have been associated with the passage of time, both the time of day and the time of year. The latter was particularly important, just as it is today, for man needed to know the seasons of the year

accurately, in order to know when to sow, when to gather in the harvest, when to prepare for the onset of winter, and when to expect storms and floods. A wooden staff or pole driven into the ground in a vertical position would have been the simplest form of indicator or gnomon which would have enabled man to determine such information from the direction and length of its shadow. The earliest recorded reference to a sundial goes back to the year 1300 BC in Egypt, while the earliest known Graeco-Roman sundial has been dated at 300 BC.

A mosaic panel in the floor of the Roman villa at Brading in the Isle of Wight, depicting a scene in which there is the earliest representation of a sundial in Britain, c.AD 250.

Left and below: *The Bewcastle Cross, Cumbria, is regarded as one of the finest works of late seventh-century Anglo-Saxon art. The earliest known sundial to be made in Britain is carved about two-thirds of the way up the shaft (close-up view below). The style hole, from which the hour lines radiate, would once have had a wooden or metal peg inserted into it, to project at right-angles to the dial as an indicator or gnomon. The dial shows both the twenty-four-hour time system and the old octaval tide system, indicating the canonical hours, used to determine the times of church services. The ornamental vine scrolls decorating the shaft of what was once a massive cross show a Mediterranean influence.*

Most people think of a sundial as being the common or garden horizontal sundial and see it simply as a garden ornament rather than as an instrument for determining the time. However, for centuries in Britain vertical wall sundials were probably more common than any other form of dial and served both to regulate public clocks and to indicate the time to the passer-by. Sundials take many forms, shapes and sizes, but the vertical dial appears to have been the first fixed basic dial to have been in use in Britain. The earliest known dial of this kind can be seen on the Bewcastle Cross, in a remote churchyard in

A Graeco-Roman vertical sundial of the kind from which the earliest British sundials may have been derived. It is situated at the corner of the south transept of the church at Orchomenos, Boeotia, in Greece, and may be of a later date than the Bewcastle dial. It is numbered from one to ten in Greek alphabetical numerals.

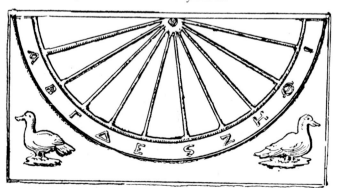

The Celtic or Cymric sundial of St Beuno's church at Clynnog-fawr, Gwynedd, thought to date from about the eighth or ninth century, is one of the earliest recorded dials in Britain. It is incised at the head of a flat oblong free-standing stone, over 6 feet (1.9 metres) in height, delineated in the 'seasonal' system to indicate the canonical hours from sunrise to sunset (6 a.m. to 6 p.m.).

Cumbria, north of Hadrian's Wall and close by the remains of a Roman fort. Only the shaft of the cross remains, but it represents one of the finest surviving examples of Anglo-Saxon sculpture. It is elaborately decorated with carved panels and shows a strong Mediterranean influence. The date of the cross is uncertain, but, from the evidence of the extensive runic inscriptions and from the quality of the sculpture, which suggests that it was a product of the golden age of Anglo-Saxon art, it probably dates from the late seventh century, about 685. The sundial itself also shows signs of Mediterranean influence. Indeed, the knowledge and skills required to construct the dial must almost certainly have had Near Eastern or Graeco-Roman scientific cultural origins. The sundial takes the form of a semicircle, with a style hole at the centre, from which a series of downward radiating lines extends to the circumference. Originally a style or gnomon, in the form of a wooden or metal peg, would have been fixed in the style hole, projecting at right-angles to the vertical dial face towards the south. In sunlight, the shadow of the gnomon passing over the radiating lines would mark the time from sunrise to sunset. The lines divide the dial into twelve parts or hours of daylight, evidently in a system where there were twenty-four divisions counted in one day, measured from sunrise to sunrise.

It has been supposed that the Anglo-Saxons also used an octaval or tide system of time measurement, whereby the twenty-four-hour day was divided into eight parts or *tides*, each of three hours duration. The word 'tide' is derived from the Anglo-Saxon term for time or

A late Anglo-Saxon dial on St Mary's church at North Stoke, Oxfordshire. Note the iron gnomon projecting from the dial and the hour lines, marked with a cross, denoting the principal church services of the day.

The vertical Anglo-Saxon dial, dated to the late seventh or early eighth century, set high up in the wall of St Michael's church, Winchester. The dial is carved out of a square block of stone and is contained within a double circle with ornamental fleur-de-lis at each corner. There are similar dials at Corhampton and Warnford, both in Hampshire.

hour. The terms 'morningtide', 'noontide' and 'eventide' are still occasionally used. However, the Christian church kept a strict system of its own to mark the regular times of prayer, according to the hours of the offices arising from the Passion of Christ. These church offices were at three-hour intervals, which were known as *canonical hours*. Of special significance were the third, sixth and ninth hours and it is clear that many Anglo-Saxon sundials were constructed primarily for the purpose of indicating these particular times or tides, since the corresponding hour lines are usually marked with a cross at their extremity. In addition to the duodecimal (twelve-division) hour system, the dial on the Bewcastle Cross is also marked in this manner for these three church offices. Thus, the Bewcastle dial is not only the first known prime-vertical sundial in Britain, constructed for the technical determination of time, but also the first ecclesiastical dial for the measurement of church offices.

Anglo-Saxon sundials should not be confused with those dials more commonly found scratched on the walls of churches,

A typical 'scratch' dial or mass dial carved into the south-facing wall of Yanworth church, Gloucestershire. Originally the dial was probably painted on the limewashed wall of the church and scored over by successive priests, to mark out the hours of the services, before repainting. Note the other small dial and carving at the bottom left of the picture.

Above: *The principle of the mass dial: a pencil has been inserted into the style hole, which originally would probably have contained a wooden peg, projecting perpendicularly to the wall on which the dial is carved. Like the hour hand of a clock, the shadow indicates the times of the services, but, like the earlier Anglo-Saxon sundials, it is accurate only at midday.*

Above: *Another example of a mass or scratch dial.*

and known as *scratch dials* or *mass dials*. These are usually crudely scored into the stonework and are generally of a later date. Several such dials are often found close together on the same wall and it is supposed that they were the work of individual clerics, scoring the wall so that when the church was limewashed, as was once a practice, a small sundial could be painted and repainted readily, to mark the times of the church services. The Anglo-Saxon sundials, however, as well as being technical instruments, were, in many cases, finely produced works of art. By comparison with the number of recorded scratch dials that have survived over the years (about four thousand), Anglo-Saxon dials are rare, but a number of beautiful examples can still be seen and appreciated. Bishopstone, in East Sussex, has a fine but simple Anglo-Saxon dial, probably dating from around 950, which, like Bewcastle, is marked for both the duodecimal system of time measurement and for the primary ecclesiastical offices. However, St Gregory's Minster at Kirkdale in North Yorkshire has what is regarded as the best example of an Anglo-Saxon dial that has come down to us. It is considered to date from about 1064 and is in an excellent state of preservation, because a porch was built on to the building at a later date and has reduced the effects of wind and weather.

These Anglo-Saxon vertical sundials and the early medieval mass dials or scratch dials were far from being accurate. The

The vertical Anglo-Saxon sundial at St Gregory's Minster, Kirkdale, North Yorkshire, dating from about 1064. The dial shows the octaval 'tide' system of time measurement, indicating the canonical hours that regulated the times of church services. The most important of these are marked by a small cross at the extremity of the hour line.

primary cause of this was the use of a horizontal gnomon, which would have been perfectly satisfactory for a dial at or near the equator, but which would not give accurate readings in the higher latitudes of northern Europe or Britain. Only with the introduction of what might be described as the scientific sundial, with a gnomon inclined parallel to the axis of the earth,

The very early scientific 'mass' sundial on the west corner of the south wall of St Mary's church at Selling, Kent. This dial has been incised as a direct-south instrument; but, to achieve this, the stone itself or the 'dial block' has been cut away to allow for the declination of the wall (about 8 degrees towards the east). The dial probably dates from the early sixteenth century but appears to have been re-incised at a later date, perhaps in the seventeenth century. Both Roman and Arabic numerals can be detected, while the remains of an iron gnomon and old leadwork are still visible.

The title page of the first book in English to be devoted to sundials, written by Thomas Fale and published in London in 1593.

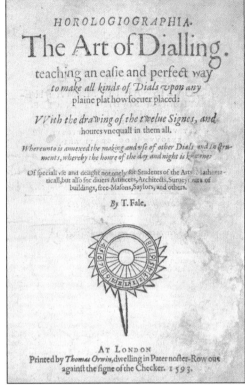

HOROLOGIOGRAPHIA.

The Art of Dialling.

teaching an easie and perfect way *to make all kinds of Dials vpon any* plaine plat howfoeuer placed:

VVith the drawing of the twelue Signes, and houres vnequall in them all.

Whereunto is annexed the making and vfe of other Dials and Inftru-ments, whereby the houre of the day and night is knowne:

Of speciall vfe and delight not onely for Students of the Arts Mathema-ticall, but alfo for diuers Artificers, Architects, Surueyours of buildings, free-Mafons, Saylors, and others.

By T. Fale.

AT LONDON
Printed by *Thomas Orwin,* dwelling in Pater nofter-Row out againft the figne of the Checker. 1 5 9 3.

and which showed hours of equal length throughout the year, did the determination of time become a functional science. While the technical benefits of inclining the gnomon parallel to the earth's axis may have been realised as early as the first century AD, it was not until the early eleventh century that the theory of equal hours was developed on a practical basis by the Arabs, who are thought to have devised the prototype of the 'modern' sundial in the late twelfth or early thirteenth century. How and when this fundamental advance in the science of gnomonics was transmitted to Britain is unknown. It might have been during the Crusades, around the twelfth century, when northern European nations were brought into direct contact with Arabian science and culture, or through Moorish influence in Spain.

In the thirteenth century mechanical clocks that sounded and showed twenty-four equal hours were coming into use. While such clocks were complementary to the sundial, showing hours of equal length, they were unreliable and needed to be frequently checked. It was the sundial that served this purpose. By the fifteenth century, with the coming of the Renaissance, the division of the day into twenty-four equal hours had come into common use. Clocks and sundials flourished side by side, the one giving the time in cloudy weather and during hours of darkness, the other providing the means to regulate the clock, by determining the time of day from the position of the sun, during periods of sunshine. Over the next four hundred years, both clocks and sundials were produced in great profusion. Sundials, both portable and fixed, appeared in much variety and complexity, not out of necessity, but for artistic pleasure and to prove the mathematical skills and ingenuity of the diallist.

During the Renaissance the science of gnomonics, or the art of dialling as it was more generally known in Britain, became established as an important mathematical subject, closely related to astronomy and navigation, and its understanding was an accepted academic accomplishment in colleges and universities. Particular impetus was given to this dynamic science by the advent of the movable-type printing press in the latter half of the fifteenth century, enabling the knowledge of this subject to be readily communicated. The earliest printed treatises on gnomonics appeared in Germany, France and Italy. The first work in English devoted to sundials was published in London in 1593 under the title *Horologiographia: The Art of Dialling* by Thomas Fale, a Cambridge mathematician. Thereafter, the publication of English dialling works grew steadily, just as the art of dialling itself progressed from the sixteenth century and flourished throughout the seventeenth and eighteenth centuries. Only with the greatly increased accuracy of mechanical timekeepers and the development of railways in the nineteenth century did the usefulness of the sundial decline. Even at the beginning of the twentieth century a number of mechanical sundials were produced for use in areas where no time checks were readily available. Indeed, an advertisement for a sundial, intended as a functional instrument, for the serious purpose of determining time in remote places, was advertised as late as 1934 in the *Nautical Almanac*. Modern communications have now placed the art of dialling, as a scientific subject, into the history books. Nevertheless, this ancient art is part of our heritage and its study can give much pleasure.

A modern vertical direct-west dial on the church of St Margaret of Antioch, Westminster. Note that the gnomon lies parallel to the dial plate, both being parallel to the earth's polar axis. The dial is one of four, which overlook Parliament Square and Westminster Abbey. They are painted blue, with the numerals gilded in platinum, and were designed by the author. They were made by Brookbrae Ltd of London in 1982.

Vertical dials

Since vertical sundials, set up on walls in public places to regulate clocks and to give the passer-by the time of day, were the most easily seen, they were also the most common dials in general use. Some were quite plain, while others were extremely ornate. They were made of stone, slate or wood and were then fixed to the wall, or in many cases they were simply delineated directly on to the wall itself and painted. A vertical dial, set on a wall to face due south (that is, being delineated on the plane of the *prime vertical* circle), would be classed as a primary sundial and termed a *south* dial, or a *direct-south* dial, or more particularly an *erect direct-south* dial. The calculations for such a dial are simple and straightforward, as are the calculations for the other vertical primary dials, which face the cardinal points of the compass, namely a *direct-north* dial, a *direct-east* dial and a *direct-west* dial. Nowadays, dials are often referred to as 'direct-south-facing', 'direct-east-facing' and so on, but the older dialling terminology was the language of dial-makers in the centuries when dials were common everyday instruments and is more properly used.

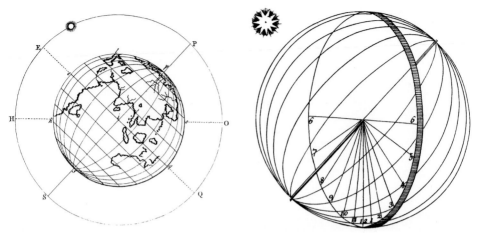

Above left: *The principles of dialling: the vertical direct-south dial. The illustration shows the theory for the construction of a prime vertical sundial for a person in Scotland. One must imagine the earth as the terrestrial sphere, at the centre of the heavens, that is the celestial sphere. One must further imagine that the terrestrial grid system of meridians and parallels of latitude can be projected on to or have their exact counterparts on the celestial sphere, except that the one system rotates within the other, about the earth's polar axis. To an observer viewing this from the centre of the earth, however, if this were possible, it would seem that the celestial system rotated about the earth. In these systems: l is the person or place in Scotland; l–o is the latitude of the place; H–O is the observer's horizon, rationalised to become a great circle on a plane passing through the centre of the earth (and the centre of the celestial sphere); e–q is the plane of the equator; E–Q is the plane of the equinoctial; P–S is the polar axis. In this diagram both systems have been stopped at a point where the sun is on the observer's meridian: in other words it is noon.*

Above right: *The principles of dialling: the vertical direct-south dial. Imagine the earth being infinitely small at the centre of the celestial sphere and imagine a vertical dial of infinite size, delineated on the plane of that great circle called the prime vertical, extending out to the celestial sphere. The sun is on the sundial's 12 o'clock meridian (it is midday for the person in Scotland and he has the sun due south of him). The gnomon of the dial is aligned and coincides exactly with the polar axis. The meridian circles are all great circles whose planes cut the polar axis and the poles at 15 degree intervals. By projecting the planes of the meridians on to the plane of the dial plate, the hours can be marked off.*

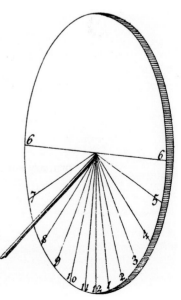

Right: *The principles of dialling: the vertical direct-south dial. Imagine the celestial sphere removed and the dial to be of normal size. This is the vertical direct-south dial, in its simplest form, which will show equal hours in the time-measuring system which is universally used today, delineated for the latitude of the person in Scotland. The theory for all other dials is based on these principles.*

A fine vertical direct-south sundial, bearing the date 1695, high up on the chimney of Morden College in Blackheath, London. The gnomon is fixed directly on the twelve o'clock hour line.

Walls seldom face directly towards a cardinal compass point and consequently most vertical sundials are not direct but *decline* or face away from the compass point by so many degrees of arc. This angle of *declination* is always measured from due north or due south away towards the east or west. Sundials that decline in this way are classed as secondary dials, and they are more complicated to calculate and to delineate than primary dials. A dial that declines from the south towards the east is termed a *south-east vertical declining dial*, or a *south-east decliner*. Likewise, a dial declining from the north towards the west is termed a *north-west decliner*, and so on. A dial with a very large declination, that is one that faces almost east or west, is termed a *great decliner*. Sometimes, perhaps for the pleasure of making the dial or simply out of vanity, the diallist would construct a *double-declining* dial, which consists of two declining dials, where one direct dial would have been sufficient. An example

Restored many times over the years, the direct-south sundial, bearing the date 1578, on the chapel of King's College, Cambridge.

Above left: *The seventeenth-century-style reconstructed direct-south sundial, designed by the author, on the south wall of the Martin Tower in the Tower of London. The restoration was carried out by Plowden & Smith Ltd of London.*

Above right: *The restored direct-south vertical dial on Ripon Cathedral, North Yorkshire.*

A restored early-eighteenth-century sundial (c.1731) on the church of St Mary and St Margaret at Castle Bromwich, Warwickshire.

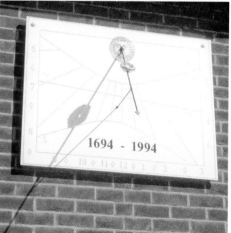

A modern south-facing vertical sundial on Thomas Philipot's Almshouses in Eltham, south-east London, designed by the author and commissioned to mark the three-hundredth anniversary of the foundation of the original almshouses in 1694. The dial was made by Brookbrae Ltd of London.

Above: An eighteenth-century direct-south sundial on a Devon church. The dial has been wedged out from the wall (which declines some 20 degrees to the west) in order to set it to face due south. Since it was easier to calculate and make a direct-south vertical sundial than it was to construct a declining dial, wedging the dial out in this manner helped to resolve the problem.

Above: *An eighteenth-century vertical declining mural sundial, dated 1783, painted on the south-east wall of the old toll-gate house in Ledbury, Herefordshire.*

Right: *A curious vertical sundial, probably seventeenth-century, on the porch of Yanworth church in Gloucestershire. It has evidently been carved from a single block of stone, as a direct-south vertical dial, and oriented in situ, before being set in place into the wall. The hour lines are marked with Arabic numerals.*

A modern mural sundial, designed by the author, on the curved south wall of the Argos building in Wimbledon, London. It was made by Brookbrae Ltd of London in 1996.

A vertical north-west 'great decliner' on the west-facing corner of a building in Cheapside, in the City of London. The term 'great decliner' applies because the wall on which the dial is situated declines some 75 degrees of arc from the north cardinal point of the compass towards the west. As a result of this large declination, the hour lines are closely bunched together, while the dial centre, from which the hour lines are delineated, is off the dial plate altogether. The dial shows the local apparent time to be about 3 p.m.

An eighteenth-century double-declining vertical sundial on the wall above the south porch of St Peter's church at Evercreech, Somerset. The dial plates each decline by 45 degrees, facing south-east and south-west respectively. Note the parallel styles of the iron gnomons, lying in the polar axis of the earth.

of this may be seen on St Peter's church at Evercreech, Somerset, probably put up in the eighteenth century. More rarely, one may come across a dial that combines perhaps three or four declining dials, on a square stone block, perhaps mounted above a porch, but of less practical use and certainly constructed as a 'conceit'.

SUNDIAL FURNITURE

Sundials, particularly vertical sundials, frequently indicate much more than just the hour of the day. They were often designed to give such information as the position of the sun in the zodiac (that is the date), the azimuth of the sun, the altitude of the sun, the number of hours elapsed since sunrise (sometimes called *Babylonian hours*), the number of hours elapsed since sunset on the previous evening (sometimes called *Italian hours*) and much more besides. This additional information, with which a dial may be furnished, is known as the *furniture* of the dial. To impress people, if not to expound

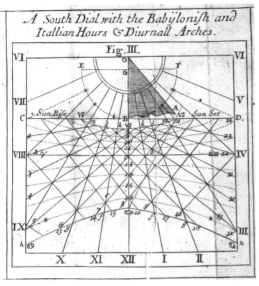

A direct-south dial with its furniture (from 'Leybourn's Dialling Improv'd' by Henry Wilson, London, 1721). The dial illustrated shows the mathematical embellishments or furniture that could be applied to a basic sundial. Babylonian hours, so called, are the hours that have elapsed since sunrise, measured from the left-hand side of the horizontal line C–D, in a series of twenty-four hours from sunrise to sunrise. Italian hours, so called, are the hours that have elapsed since sunset on the previous evening, measured from the right-hand side of the horizontal line C–D, in a series of twenty-four hours from sunset to sunset. The diurnal arches are the lines which mark the sun's declination, or angular distance north or south of the equator. The movement of the gnomon's shadow or projected spot of light along these lines can indicate the date and sign of the zodiac in which the sun is situated.

the mathematical complexities of dialling, dial-makers would sometimes fill sundials with such furniture, often making them difficult to read. In the Time Garden in Carnfunnock Country Park at Larne in Northern Ireland there are some modern vertical sundials that demonstrate the use of individual items of dialling furniture and show that they are quite easy to understand.

At Green College, Oxford, there is a dial that shows only the twelve o'clock hour line and indicates the moment of noon, when the sun is on the meridian. This moment has always been

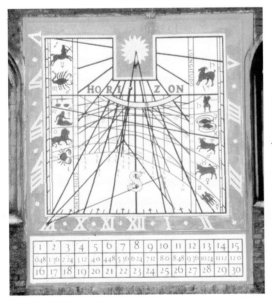

The famous sundial on the south wall of the Old Court, Queens' College, Cambridge. It is adorned with a multitude of furniture, so that the shadow of a small spherical 'nodus', being an integral part of the gnomon, will indicate not only the hour of the day, but also the sun's 'azimuth' or direction, its 'altitude' or angular height above the horizon, the times of its rising and setting, the date or the sign of the zodiac, and a wealth of other information, including its use as a moon dial, with the help of the table of corrections below the dial. It has been said that Sir Isaac Newton was responsible for the design of the sundial.

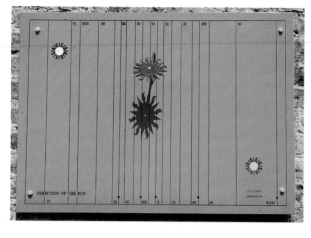

One of the modern wall dials designed by the author to illustrate the furniture of a sundial and made by Brookbrae Ltd of London. These dials may be seen in Carnfunnock Park 'Time Garden' at Larne, Northern Ireland. By means of a spot of light, projected by the nodus at the centre of the sun-image gnomon on to the dial plate, this dial indicates the azimuth or compass bearing of the sun, that is, its direction. In this case it indicates the bearing to be about 15 degrees from south towards the east, i.e. south-south-east (about an hour before midday.)

Another of the modern wall dials in the Time Garden at Larne designed by the author and made by Brookbrae Ltd. It indicates the time by the old unequal seasonal hour or planetary hour system.

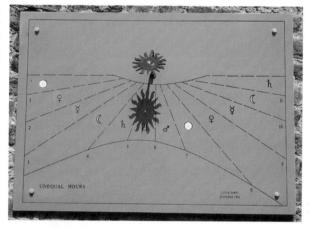

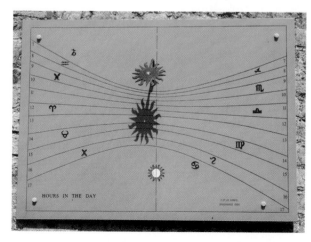

A third dial in the same series in the Time Garden at Larne. This sundial shows the length of the day ('longitudo dierum') in terms of the number of equal hours in the day between sunrise and sunset. The spot of light at the centre of the shadow of the sun-image gnomon indicates that there are some 13 hours 55 minutes in the day, which is consistent with the date when the photograph was taken on 29th August 1992. It will be observed that the sun is in the zodiacal sign of Virgo.

An ornate vertical declining sundial (facing 18 degrees west of south) on the wall of the parish church of St Lawrence in Eyam, Derbyshire. Dated 1775, it was designed by Mr Duffin, clerk at nearby Stoke Hall, and executed by William Shore, a local stonemason. Fitted with an iron gnomon, it is a large dial, 5 feet (1.5 metres) square, of exceptional quality, well delineated and displaying an array of seemingly complex furniture. It also indicates the time of 12 o'clock (noon) at different places around the world, including Mecca, Constantinople, Quebec and Panama.

A fine slate sundial on the south wall above the porch of St Peter's church at Tawstock in north Devon, dated 1757 and signed by its maker, John Berry. In addition to the usual furniture, it also displays lines of demarcation between the six celestial 'houses' above the horizon, enabling the observer to determine in which of the twelve diurnal 'houses', pertaining to astrology, the sun may be found at any time during the course of the day. These lines represent the projection of the great circles of the celestial sphere called 'domifying circles', or more commonly 'circles of position'.

of great importance, since it provides the one instant during each day when the sun is at a known reference point and hence provides the basis for the determination of time during the twenty-four-hour solar day. To this end, the *noon mark* (sundial) was sometimes used to provide a daily time check, rather than by the use of the more conventional dial. Furthermore, the noon-mark dial could be furnished with the equation of time correction curve (or *analemma*), which

A very large modern mural sundial on the Director's house, which was built as part of the Przypkowski Public State Museum, containing the historic Przypkowski family gnomonical instrument collection and sundial library, at Jedrzejow in Poland. The Director, Dr Tadeusz Przypkowski, is seen here, in 1969, standing below one of his many splendid mural sundials, which is adorned with simple but dramatic zodiacal furniture. The shadow of a symbolic rose-shaped gnomon, with a small disc of light at its centre, projected by a circular aperture nodus, indicates the date to be about 25th October and the time to be about 3.15 p.m. local apparent time.

Left: *A modern vertical declining glass-window noon mark and mean-time sundial, designed by Douglas Bateman, in the headquarters building of QINETIQ at Farnborough, Hampshire, formerly the Defence Evaluation and Research Agency and before that the Royal Aircraft Establishment. It can be easily read from both inside and outside the building, indicating not only mean-time noon, but also local apparent noon and the date, with considerable accuracy.*

Right: *A vertical noon-mark dial, delineated with only the 12 o'clock hour line, as illustrated in Bedos de Celles's work 'La Gnomonique Pratique', first published in Paris in 1760. The gentlemen are checking their watches, observing the moment when the spot of light, projecting the sun's rays through a small nodus at the centre of the gnomon (the 'solar' disk supported by a tripod), is exactly on the noon line.*

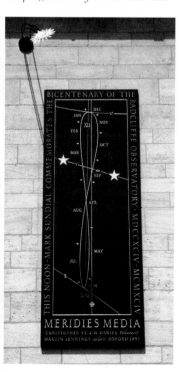

A modern vertical declining noon mark and mean-time sundial (Meridies Media), designed by the author and superbly executed in slate by Martin Jennings, at Green College, Oxford. The gnomon takes the form of a gilded sun image with a small circular aperture at its centre (the nodus), through which the sun's rays are projected, as a spot of light, on to the dial plate. When the spot of light crosses the figure-of-eight equation of time correction curve (the analemma), according to the date, the dial will indicate 12 o'clock noon Greenwich Mean Time (GMT), or 1 p.m. British Summer Time (BST) when summer time is in force. When the spot of light crosses the central vertical noon line, it will be 12 o'clock noon, local apparent time, when the sun will be on the meridian of Oxford.

enabled *local mean time* to be read directly off the dial. The Green College noon dial is furnished in this manner and thus demonstrates the means by which clock time can be obtained. In this case, being at Oxford, the correction curve is offset to allow for the difference in longitude from the prime meridian at Greenwich and hence shows GMT. In fact, most sundials can be corrected for the difference in longitude (that is, the time difference between the standard time zone meridian and that of the sundial) and can be furnished with equation of time curves for all hours. Such dials are rare, although fine modern examples, the work of the Reverend Father George Fenech, may be seen on a number of churches in Malta.

STAINED-GLASS SUNDIALS

Of all the common vertical sundials, the least common and the most beautiful are the stained-glass sundials that were built into the windows of mansions and churches in the seventeenth century and occasionally later. In these dials may be seen the mathematical skills of the diallist combined with the talents of

the glass-painter. The dials are calculated and delineated in exactly the same way as for ordinary vertical dials, direct or declining, except that they are made of glass and built into a suitably situated window. The gnomon is fitted on the outside of the window, but the numerals are reversed and read from the inside, so that the viewer need not leave the comfort of the room on a sunny but cold winter's day.

Stained-glass dials became popular in the latter part of

Above: A beautiful rare seventeenth-century south-east declining glass-window sundial at Berkeley Castle, Gloucestershire. Note the painted fly, an ornamental feature frequently found on stained-glass dials, seemingly being a glass-painter's pun on 'time flies'.

The earliest known stained-glass sundial in England, an exquisite little roundel only 2¾ inches (7 cm) in diameter, signed by the artist Bernard Dininckhoff and dated 1585, set into the magnificent heraldic window in the Great Chamber of Gilling Castle, North Yorkshire.

Above left: *Perhaps the most famous of all stained-glass sundials, depicting a bird, probably a skylark, on the branch of a tree looking at a fly as a prospective meal! The winged hourglass, within the framework of the glass oval medallion, and the motto 'Dum spectas fugio' ('Whilst you watch, I fly') reinforce the message that 'time flies' and that life is short. The dial has been variously dated at c.1620 and (more probably) 1660 and was evidently made originally for a manor house in Devon. For many years it was in a window at Nailsea Court in Somerset but has since disappeared. The dial was copied for an office in Derby in 1888 by Frederick Drake of Exeter, while sketches and drawings of the copy appear in numerous publications. A copy has been reproduced by glaziers in New York.*

Above right: *A simple and beautiful glass-window dial, depicting a cornflower, at Gray's Court, York, attributed to the well-known glass-painter Henry Gyles of York (1645–1709).*

the seventeenth century, when puritan prejudice against colourful windows in churches obliged glass-painters to look elsewhere for business, towards secular buildings, such as university colleges, civic halls, city mansions and the country houses of the landed gentry. One noted glass-painter, Henry

Probably the finest complete glass sundial, undamaged and with the gnomon intact, at Tong Hall, near Bradford, West Yorkshire, also attributed to and wholly typical of the work of Henry Gyles.

A modern stained-glass sundial in seventeenth-century-style, designed by the author and made by the York Glaziers' Trust in 1998 for the chapel of the Merchant Adventurers' Hall in York. It depicts a young sea-going gentleman, standing on the deck of a ship and using a cross-staff to measure the equinoctial meridian altitude of the sun in order to obtain the latitude.

Gyles of York (1645–1709), apparently appealed to his friend Francis Place, the well-known London engraver, who replied: 'I made Inquiry at Mr Price's about glass painters: he tells me there is 4 In Towne but not enough work to Imploy one, if he did nothing Else.' Nevertheless, as a result of this sad state of affairs, the glass-painter became more creative in his designs, turning from biblical scenes to heraldry, history, portraiture and so on, including glass sundials.

Since they are made of glass, there are not many of these dials in existence. Over the years, many have been broken or removed and they have usually disappeared without trace. The glass was thin and fragile, and it had to be drilled through in two or three places to allow the gnomon to be fixed in position. Consequently, it is fortunate that there are any examples at all of these glass sundials left.

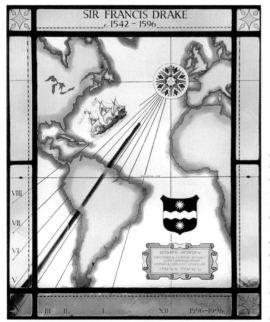

A modern vertical declining stained-glass sundial, designed by the author and made by Goddard & Gibbs of London for Buckland Abbey (National Trust) in Devon, to commemorate the four-hundredth anniversary of the death of Sir Francis Drake. The dial declines by 66 degrees from the south towards the west and represents a sixteenth-century period chart of the Atlantic, with Drake's famous ship, the 'Golden Hinde', on the 8 o'clock evening hour line, on course from Plymouth to Porto Bello, where he died and was buried at sea in 1596.

Left: *A typical 'stumped cross' pillar dial in Somerset. In 1644 the puritan troops of Cromwell's army broke off the cross, once a preaching cross, showing their disapproval of the established church. After the Restoration many such monuments were given a sundial in place of a cross, to serve a more utilitarian purpose.*

Below: *A practical eighteenth-century pillar sundial in the grounds of Houghton Hall, Norfolk.*

PILLAR SUNDIALS

During the reign of Queen Elizabeth I in the sixteenth century there was a Protestant backlash against the previous reign of the Catholic Mary, and some town and village preaching crosses were desecrated, for they were seen as symbols of the Roman Catholic religion. Likewise, during the Civil War, which began in 1642, many surviving crosses were reduced to stumps by the Parliamentarian troops. Again, they were seen as symbols of a wealthy church that supposedly supported the monarchy. The crosses had been set up originally to remind the traveller of his Christian beliefs and to encourage him to give prayers of thanksgiving for

A fine classical eighteenth-century pillar sundial on The Green in York, close to the Minster.

The market-cross pillar sundial at Witney, Oxford-shire, set up in 1685.

his safe arrival at each stage of his journey. They also served as meeting places, where clergy could preach to a congregation if there were no church, or where people could simply voice their opinions. Frequently they were set up in market places at the centre of the town and were referred to as market crosses.

Despite the turbulent times, the art of dialling flourished, and it was this art that provided a use for the stumped cross. By placing a stone block on which a dial or dials had been carved on top of the pillar where the cross itself had been, the structure was restored as an object of dignity, if not of religious significance. Thus the 'cross', particularly the market cross, continued to serve as a meeting place, with the added benefit of a sundial to tell the time of day. Many of these crosses were roofed over, to give shelter from the weather, but some new seventeenth-century market crosses were purposely built to support a sundial. Such a dial would usually take the form of a direct-south sundial, or, if more than one dial was provided, they would be direct vertical dials, which were easily placed to face the cardinal points of the compass. Oakham in Rutland and Witney and Woodstock in Oxfordshire, for example, each had a

The twentieth-century William Willett memorial pillar sundial, set up in 1927 in Petts Wood, Kent, commemorating the institution of British Summer Time.

The historic pillar sundial overlooking the busy A66 road, just east of Brougham Castle, near Penrith in Cumbria. It is known as the 'Countess's Pillar', having been erected in 1656 by Anne Clifford, Dowager Countess of Pembroke (1590–1675), as a memorial of her last parting from her mother at this spot forty years earlier. The north face of the dial block bears the arms appertaining to the Clifford family, while the south, east and west faces bear direct-facing dials. Anne Clifford was an outstanding and celebrated lady, who successfully fought for her rights and those of her people before, during and after the Civil War.

market cross of this kind, although the only trace of the Woodstock cross is a stone remnant, supposedly the actual dial, built into the wall of the town hall.

With the Restoration of the Monarchy in 1660, the art of dialling continued to flourish and increase in popularity. Elegant dials were made and mounted in conspicuous places to indicate the time. In the same spirit, pillar dials were built with classical grace as primary features of villages, towns and cities. Although many such dials were pulled down long ago, notably the famous Seven Dials and Covent Garden dials in London, there are still a number of fine examples to be seen throughout Britain.

At East Hagbourne near Didcot in Oxfordshire there is a typical example of a seventeenth-century stumped-cross dial, while York has a 'classical' pillar dial of the late seventeenth or early eighteenth century (albeit with the gnomon of the north dial fixed in the wrong way). Other remarkable detached pillar dials include the one known as the Countess's Pillar, a massive column set up in 1656 by Anne Clifford, Countess of Pembroke, at a lonely spot on the wayside between Brougham and Appleby in Cumbria, and the roadside dial at Chippenham causeway, Wiltshire, set up in 1698.

Multiple dials

While the basic utilitarian dial for public purposes was the common vertical sundial, the art of dialling bloomed in sixteenth- and seventeenth-century Britain in many complex mathematical forms, which were particularly manifested in *multiple* sundials. These were usually but not always *detached* dials, as were pillar dials, that is, they were not attached to a building. The evidence suggests that the earliest English multiple sundials may have had their origins in Germany and France. A German scholar and astronomer, Nicolaus Kratzer, came to England, perhaps in early 1518, to the court of Henry VIII to be appointed 'deviser of the King's *horologes*' (sundials). Furthermore, there are interesting similarities between the dials illustrated in the works of Sebastian Munster, an eminent gnomonical authority, and the earliest known multiple dials in England, which are probably those at Elmley Castle, Worcestershire, possibly dating from about 1545. Nicolaus Kratzer set up an elaborate pillar multiple dial outside St Mary's church, Oxford, in about 1523, and another in the garden of Corpus Christi College nearby. Although almost all colleges had their own sundials, few sixteenth-century examples survive and Kratzer's dials had disappeared by the early eighteenth century. However, the restored Turnbull Dial, often called the Pelican Dial, which stands in the front quadrangle of Corpus Christi, is a beautiful example of an early multiple dial although it is not the original dial of 1579.

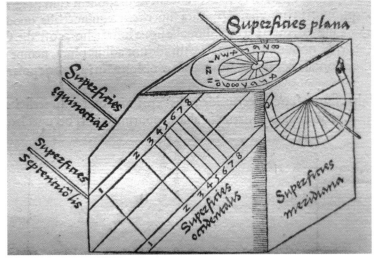

A woodcut in 'Horologio-graphia', published in Basel, Switzerland, in 1533, an early work on sundials by Sebastian Munster (1489–1552). Although it does not show any scaphe dials, it illustrates the popular form of the cuboid multiple sundial.

The famous column in Corpus Christi College, Oxford, known as the Turnbull Dial. It is a multiple sundial, originally set up in the sixteenth century.

A multiple dial, as the term implies, is a sundial that comprises numerous individual dials as component parts of the sundial as a whole. For the most part, multiple dials were intended for decorative purposes to show off the mathematical knowledge and skills of

Above: *The multiple sundial, mounted on a pedestal, in the churchyard of St Mary's church, Old Eastbourne, East Sussex. The sundial comprises a limestone block in the form of a polyhedral cuboid, with six or possibly seven plane dials on the visible faces, together with some five scaphe dials cut into the various surfaces. Traces of the original iron gnomons can be seen where they have been leaded in to the stonework. The origin of the dial is obscure and its date is uncertain, but it is probably early-sixteenth-century since it has a striking resemblance to a stone sundial bearing the date 1520 which may be attributed to Nicolaus Kratzer (1486–1550) and is similar in form to a woodcut in Sebastian Munster's 'Horologiographia' of 1533.*

Right: *The earliest dated multiple sundial still in situ, in the grounds of Marrington Hall, Chirbury, Shropshire. It takes the form of a beautifully carved rectangular granite column, incorporating eleven component dials, including a horizontal dial, dated 1595.*

Above left: *A multiple sundial in the churchyard of St Mary's church, Elmley Castle, Worcestershire. Although much of it has been restored, it is perhaps the earliest dial of its kind in England, thought to date from about 1545. Note the hollowed scaphe dials.*

Above right: *A tall and impressive stone multiple sundial in the grounds of Great Fosters (now an hotel) at Egham, Surrey. The dial block takes the form of an octagonal prism, about 2 feet (61 cm) in diameter and 10 inches (25 cm) thick, which has similarities with the portable sundial devised for Cardinal Wolsey by Nicolaus Kratzer. Comprising eighteen component dials, including numerous incised scaphes, the sundial is mounted on a pillar standing on a large rectangular pedestal and is surmounted by a short cylindrical column, which once supported a weathervane. The sundial, by popular tradition, is referred to as 'Sir Francis Drake's Dial' and is thought to date from c.1585–90.*

The massive 4 foot (122 cm) stone cube multiple sundial at Madeley Court (now an hotel) in Shropshire. In addition to the crowning convex dial, it comprises fifty-six component scaphe dials, including, on three of the four sides, a 'great concave' hemispherical scaphe measuring 26 inches (66 cm) in diameter. These great concave dials would once have enabled their owner to determine a whole range of astronomical information. The sundial may well have resembled and date from the same period as the famous Whitehall dial designed by Edmond Gunter, the noted mathematician, for King James I and made in 1622 by Nicholas Stone, the eminent sculptor, for the palace privy garden.

The great multiple sundial at Upton Manor Farm, near Peterborough. Made of Ketton stone, the dial stands over 5 feet 7½ inches (1.7 metres) in overall height and is thought to have been made by Nicholas Stone, master mason to James I and Charles I, in about 1627.

the diallist. On examining such a sundial, one may find a whole range of small component dials, including almost every class of dial described – horizontal, equinoctial, polar, vertical (direct and declining) as well as inclining/proclining, reclining and deinclining dials – together with a variety of cup and scaphe dials, hollowed out of the stone in different shapes and sizes.

The remarkable 'Pyramidical Dial' which was set up in the King's Privy Garden at Whitehall on 24th June 1669. This ornate multiform or multiple sundial, standing 10 feet 3 inches (3 metres) in height, constructed of stone, brass and wood, with finely painted glass panels and gleaming with gilded ironwork, incorporated 270 component dials and was the work of the Reverend Francis Hall (alias Line), professor of mathematics at Liège University. It is preserved only in the pages of the designer's own 'Explication', published in London in 1673. By 1710 the dial was in a sad state of disrepair and was last seen at Buckingham House in London.

A seventeenth-century multiple polyhedral sundial on a pedestal in the gardens of Penshurst Place, Kent, and restored early in the second half of the twentieth century, when the twenty-four faces of the dial were fitted with new small brass gnomons. Traces of pigment on some surfaces indicate that the sundial was once colourfully painted, as was the fashion at the time.

An eighteenth-century polyhedral sundial at Penshurst Place, Kent. It illustrates the alignment of the gnomons with the polar axis. It also illustrates a polar sundial, above the vertical direct-south dial, and a direct proclining dial immediately below it, just visible in the picture.

While the earliest multiple dials to be found in England may exhibit German or French influence, the most extraordinary multiple dials are found in Scotland and their origin is a matter for speculation. Undoubtedly the Scottish mind for mathematics and science took to the multiple sundial in a way that is found nowhere else in the science of gnomonics or the art of dialling. These magnificent multiple dials are unique to Scotland and show a remarkable passion for dialling in all its most complex mathematical forms. These dials have been subdivided into classes: obelisk-shaped, lectern-shaped and facet-headed dials. The typical *obelisk* dial comprises a square stone shaft, above which is placed a bulged octagonal-shaped capital, with a tapering finial above, the whole reaching a height of about $7^1/2$ feet (2.3 metres). On every surface are incised all manner of dials, some with gnomons, others without but using the edge of a piece of stonework to cast the shadow. *Lectern* dials, as the term implies, resemble a lectern but again contain dials of all shapes and sizes. The *facet-headed* dials also

The famous multiple 'obelisk' sundial, the seventeenth-century centrepiece of the magnificent Drummond Castle gardens, near Crieff in Perthshire. It was made by John Mylne in 1630 and is one of the earliest dials in this class, which is unique to Scotland.

Above: *A modern multiple scaphe dial, set up as a memorial in 1976 in the parish churchyard of St Neot in Cornwall. The dial was designed by S. H. Grylls, who had formerly been the Chief Engineer of Rolls-Royce.*

Left: *A comparatively simple Scottish polyhedral sundial.*

contain large numbers of small dials, but, as the name implies, the bulk of these are combinations of vertical declining and inclining dials. Such an edifice sometimes resembles the ornate head of a mace, once carried into battle by knights in armour, and may contain as many as two hundred individual dials or more. The dials themselves are of no great accuracy, but they do illustrate every conceivable form of traditional dial.

Another example of a multiple obelisk-shaped sundial, in the gardens of Mountstuart, on the Isle of Bute in the Firth of Clyde. Undated, but almost certainly seventeenth-century, the majority of its component dials are principally symbolic and possibly associated with freemasonry, in an age when symbolism was something of a cult.

Horizontal dials

The common horizontal garden sundial is classed as a primary dial and is a dial described on a horizontal plane or a plane parallel to the horizon. It is normally a detached dial, set upon a plinth away from a building in a situation where it will receive the maximum amount of sunshine all the year round.

Left: *This large sundial on its four-pillared stone pedestal in Amen Court, by St Paul's Cathedral in London, is attributed to Sir Christopher Wren (1632–1723), who was not only a great architect but also a noted astronomer. The circular brass dial plate is 28 inches (71 cm) in diameter, but the most striking feature of the dial is the 2 feet (61 cm) long gnomon, with its elaborate pierced scrollwork, containing the capital letter 'D', supported by two crossed swords or daggers. Originally the dial was made for the cathedral and it is believed to have been situated outside the library, in a position to facilitate the regulation of the clock.*

Below left: *The fine eighteenth-century horizontal brass sundial, signed 'J. Bird, London', on an ornate baroque baluster pedestal at Tapeley Park in Devon. John Bird (1709–76) was an eminent London instrument-maker, noted for his exactness, who was commissioned to make large astronomical instruments for the Royal Observatory at Greenwich.*

Below: *The circular dial plate of John Bird's sundial, 9 inches (23 cm) in diameter, at Tapeley Park. Engraved to two-minute intervals, it is a plain but elegant dial with no furniture, other than a compass rose and the given latitude '51° 11'. The straight edge of the trailing shadow indicates the time to be about 9.30 a.m. local apparent time. In the afternoon the leading edge of the shadow will indicate the time.*

Horizontal sundials became fashionable in the sixteenth century in England, both as garden ornaments and as instruments for marking the passage of time. The earliest sundial of this kind in England is uncertain, although there is in existence a horizontal dial with an apparent date of 1395 crudely cut into the underside of the dial plate, on which an earlier dial had been engraved but had seemingly never been used. The style of the engraving appears to be of a later period

Left: *A common or garden eighteenth-century horizontal brass sundial, 17¾ inches (45 cm) in diameter, bearing the inscription 'Made by G. Adams at Tycho Brahe's Head, the corner of Raquet Court, Fleet Street, London', at Littlecote Park near Hungerford in Berkshire. George Adams (Senior) (c.1704–73) was working at this address from 1738 to 1757 and was one of the most important instrument-makers of his time. The dial is typically well furnished, including a compass rose and equation of time tables, enabling the observer to set his watch correctly.*

Right: *A nineteenth-century circular horizontal sundial, 15 inches (38 cm) in diameter, made by Troughton & Simms (established 1826–1922), on the battlements of St Michael's Mount in Cornwall. Note the high angle of the gnomon (angled to the latitude of 50 degrees) directed due north in the polar axis of the earth.*

An eighteenth-century circular horizontal sundial, 10 inches (25 cm) in diameter, made in 1765 by Henry Pyefinch (fl.1739–90), of Cornhill, London, on a fine baluster stone pedestal in St John's churchyard, Barbados. Note the low angle of the gnomon (angled to the latitude of 13 degrees) lying in the polar axis of the earth.

A beautifully engraved octagonal double-horizontal sundial, made about 1700, bearing the inscription 'Made by Thomas Tuttell, Mathematical Instrument maker to the King's most excellent Majesty at Charing Cross, London', at Squerryes Court, Westerham, Kent. Note the normal inclined gnomon (left), supported by a triangular piece, the vertical edge of which forms a secondary gnomon. The trailing edge of the shadow (right), cast by the inclined gnomon, indicates the local apparent solar time to be about 10.45 a.m. The vertical support to the gnomon also casts a straight shadow, the edge of which, if followed to the point where it intersects the hour line on the planispheric (stereographic) projection of the celestial sphere, corresponding to the time indicated by the dial itself, will give the position of the sun in terms of the date, declination, altitude and azimuth. Thus the dial serves a dual purpose, hence the term 'double-horizontal dial'. It was invented by William Oughtred and published in his work 'Description and Use of the Double Horizontal Dial' (London, 1636).

than the fourteenth century, more like that of the sixteenth century, and there seems to have been no good reason why this earlier dial should not have been made use of, unless an error was made in cutting the date into the metalwork, so obliging the dial-maker to start afresh on the reverse of the plate.

The National Maritime Museum has in its sundial collection, in the Royal Observatory, a fine square bronze dial dated 1582, signed by the noted

The Reverend William Oughtred (1575–1660), the brilliant English mathematician, who invented the double-horizontal sundial, as well as the general horological ring or universal equinoctial ring dial. He was held in very high esteem not only by his contemporaries but by those who came after him, but he is perhaps best known for his textbook on algebra and arithmetic, in which he introduced the symbol 'x' for multiplication.

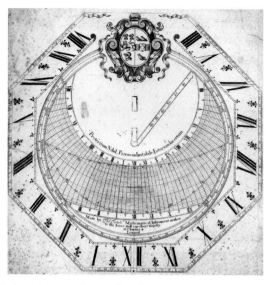

An engraving in the collections of the National Maritime Museum at Greenwich, showing a plan of the double-horizontal sundial by Thomas Tuttell. The planispheric or stereographic projection takes the form of a grid system. The sun's altitude is obtained by reference to the rule shown to the right on the dial and extending from the index of the dial support, i.e. the base of the secondary gnomon. Having determined the position of the sun on the grid, and using compasses or dividers, one measures the distance from this point to the index and compares it to the scale on the rule. Note that the equinoctial is shown on the projection, as well as the tropics of Cancer and Capricorn.

instrument-maker Humphrey Cole. A number of other examples of sixteenth-century horizontal sundials, if not still in use, are to be found in the scientific-instrument collections of various museums. Horizontal sundials have remained popular as garden ornaments to this day, being simple to read, attractive to look at and requiring little maintenance. However, during the seventeenth and eighteenth centuries, like their vertical counterparts, well-made horizontal dials were often engraved with useful furniture, including devices to give the position of the sun in the zodiac, its bearing and altitude at any moment, and the values of the equation of time. Most good instrument-makers also signed and sometimes dated their dials, which

The double-horizontal sundial at Hampton Court, Middlesex, made by Thomas Tompion (1638–1713), one of the greatest clock- and watch-makers.

A modern Arabic-style horizontal sundial, designed by the author and carved in slate by Mark Frith, presented by the Honourable Company of Master Mariners in 1995 to the UK Hydrographic Office at Taunton, Somerset, to mark the bicentenary of this organisation. It is believed to be the first sundial ever to be set in position by Global Positioning by Satellite.

Right: The great modern horizontal sundial, with stainless-steel gnomon, in Milton Keynes, Buckinghamshire.

Another great modern horizontal sundial in the centre of Plymouth, Devon.

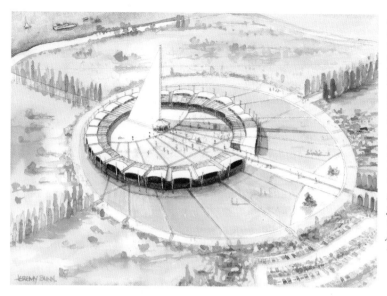

An artist's impression of the giant sundial proposed for the Greenwich peninsula to mark the Millennium, to the design of the author, with its 180 feet (55 metres) high 'landmark' stainless-steel gnomon, rejected in favour of the Dome.

Right: *The 'human' analemmatic horizontal sundial designed by the author and constructed by Brookbrae Ltd of London for the Liverpool International Garden Festival in 1984. The observer stands (as a human gnomon) on a central date scale, and his or her shadow will indicate the time, in relation to the nearest hour mark. In this case, the dial is delineated to show summer time and the shadow indicates that it is about 10 a.m., local apparent (summer) time.*

A small modern 'human' analemmatic sundial, primarily formed of mosaics, from designs by the schoolchildren, set in the playground of James Wolfe School, Greenwich, London.

The great 20 foot (6 metre) diameter 'human' sundial at the National Memorial Arboretum at Alrewas in Staffordshire. Designed by the author and executed by Mark Frith in Dunhouse stone and blue Elterwater slate, the dial represents an oval outline chart of the world, commemorating the loss of 2536 ships of the Merchant Navy and the 32,000 merchant seamen who gave their lives in the Second World War. The memorial was commissioned by the Honourable Company of Master Mariners and dedicated in 2001, marking the seventy-fifth anniversary of the founding of the Company. In the photograph, the shadow of the person standing on the date scale indicates the time to be 10.30 a.m. (local apparent time).

Left: Probably the largest horizontal analemmatic sundial in the world, in Longwood Gardens, in the United States of America. In this case, a tall vertical rod is placed in the correct position on the date scale, instead of the human gnomon, since the human shadow would not be able to reach the hour marks.

were used by their owners for the serious purpose of checking their household clocks and watches, as well as serving as centrepieces for the garden. Many of these fine dials can still be seen in the grounds of large country houses.

A seventeenth-century 'horizontal' ceiling sundial. The hour lines and declination lines, for the equinoctial and the tropics of Cancer and Capricorn, are painted on the ceiling. A spot of light, from the rays of the sun, is projected through a nodus so that it will be reflected by a small mirror on to the ceiling. Hence the time and date may be deduced from inside the building.

The most basic form of the equinoctial sundial, in which a disk is set to lie in the plane of the celestial equator (the 'equinoctial'), where the polar axis passing through its centre, perpendicular to the plane of the disk, takes the form of a rod, which is the gnomon. In the northern hemisphere, in summer, the upper surface of the disk will be illuminated and the northern extension of the gnomon rod will cast a shadow along the hour lines to indicate the time. In winter, the lower surface of the disk will be illuminated. The photograph shows such a dial, made of stone, in the courtyard of the former royal palace in Beijing, in China.

Equinoctial dials

The most important primary class of sundial, and the fundamental dial from which all others are derived, is that known as the *equinoctial* dial, that is one described on an equinoctial plane, or a plane representing that of the equinoctial. The equinoctial is the plane of the equator extended to the celestial sphere (the imagined sphere of the heavens), that is the celestial equator. It is so called because the *ecliptic* or apparent path of the sun intersects this great celestial circle at two points, and because the length of the day equals the length of the night (whence the term *equinox*) when the sun reaches one or other of these points. Thus an equinoctial dial, in its most basic form, is a flat plate or ring set to lie parallel to the plane of the equator, with a gnomon passing through its centre at right angles to the plane of the dial. Sometimes such a dial

A modern basic equinoctial sundial, by Wendy Taylor, at the entrance to St Katharine's Dock, London. Technically, it should be termed an 'upper' equinoctial dial, as it will show the time only while the sun is north of the equator.

An armillary sundial, showing the equinoctial hour ring with the shadow of the gnomon rod indicating the time to be about 2 p.m., in the grounds of Hever Castle, Kent. The various rings of the armillary dial represent the imaginary circles of the celestial sphere. The gnomon is the polar axis of this representation of the celestial sphere.

may be termed an *equatorial* dial, which is not correct in original dialling terminology but which has come to be accepted through common usage. Furthermore, the basic concept of the equinoctial dial has become extended to include those dials that have an equatorial hour ring, on which the time is indicated by the shadow of the gnomon. In this category, the *armillary* sundial is the one kind of dial that illustrates the whole principle of the science of gnomonics. It consists of a number of metal rings representing the circles of the celestial sphere, usually with a broad hour ring representing the equinoctial or celestial equator on which the numerals of each hour of the day are engraved or painted. A metal rod passes through the centre of this assembly of rings, parallel to the polar axis and

Left: A modern stainless-steel armillary sundial, designed by the author and made by Brookbrae Ltd, in the Thames Embankment gardens of the Savoy Hotel, London. It was commissioned to mark the centenary of the Savoy.

Right: *A modern gilded stainless-steel equinoctial armillary sundial, designed by the author and constructed by Brookbrae Ltd in 1999, in the centre of Windsor, Berkshire. The dial has an overall diameter of 6 feet (1.8 metres) and, on its plinth, stands at a height of about 10 feet (3 metres). In addition to indicating local apparent solar time, by the longitudinal shadow of the polar-axis rod gnomon, it also indicates the declination of the sun (and hence the date) at the moment of noon, by the use of a relatively small nodus disc, at the centre of the gnomon, the shadow of which is cast on to the inner surface of the meridian ring, graduated in degrees of declination. The mean centre line of this lateral shadow marks the date, according to the declination scale, by which a correction for the longitude and the equation of time may be applied, giving the true standard time at noon, i.e. GMT or BST.*

A seventeenth-century spherical equinoctial stone sundial, constructed for the latitude of Darlington, County Durham. With this form of dial the time was usually indicated by the 'terminator', the demarcation line between light and darkness, passing over a scale of hours incised within an equinoctial hour ring or belt around the globe. Sometimes a rod gnomon, lying in the polar axis, projecting as a spike from the north pole of the dial, would be used, to cast a shadow on to the hour scale, to indicate the time.

Right: *A modern hemispherical equinoctial sundial, designed by G. P. Woodford.*

at right-angles to the hour ring, and its shadow indicates the time. Sometimes a small metal ball is fitted at the centre of the rod, representing the earth. When the shadow of this ball passes along the centre line of the hour ring during the course of the day, provided that the dial is accurate, the sun will be at one or other of the equinoxes.

The equinoctial sundial is not only the dial least likely to be in error in its construction, but it is also the dial that lends itself most to the pursuit of accuracy, so far as accuracy may be achieved by a sundial. As clocks improved in performance, so instrument-makers sought to improve the accuracy of the sundial. In the latter part of the seventeenth century the Reverend John Flamsteed, the first Astronomer Royal at

A modern equinoctial sundial (the 'Bennoy' dial), in which the sun's rays are passed through a liquid-filled cylindrical glass gnomon, being projected on to the hour scale as an 'arrow' of light. Technically an 'upper' equinoctial dial, the instrument is graduated to show summer time.

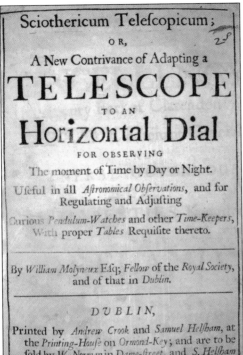

Sciothericum Telefcopicum;

O R,

A New Contrivance of Adapting a

TELESCOPE

TO AN

Horizontal Dial

FOR OBSERVING

The moment of Time by Day or Night.

Ufeful in all *Aftronomical Obfervations*, and for Regulating and Adjufting

Curious *Pendulum-Watches* and other *Time-Keepers*, With proper *Tables* Requifite thereto.

By *William Molyneux* Efq; *Fellow* of the *Royal Society*, and of that in *Dublin*.

D U B L I N,

Printed by *Andrew Crook* and *Samuel Helfham*, at the *Printing-Houfe* on *Ormond-Key*; and are to be fold by *W. Norman* in *Dame-ftreet*, and *S. Helfham* and *El. Dobfon* Bookfellers in *Caftle-ftreet*, 1686.

The title page of 'Sciothericum Telescopicum; or, A New Contrivance of Adapting a TELESCOPE to an Horizontal Dial' by William Molyneux FRS, published in Dublin in 1686. The work describes the means of fitting a large octagonal horizontal brass sundial with telescopic sights 'for observing the moment of time by day or night... and for regulating and adjusting... pendulum-watches and other time-keepers', which instrument was evidently constructed in London in the summer of 1685 by Richard Whitehead (fl.1663–93), a notable mathematical instrument-maker. This work also contains one of the earliest published tables of the equation of time, produced by John Flamsteed, the first Astronomer Royal.

Greenwich, produced an accurate table for the values of the equation of time – the difference between apparent solar time (sundial time) and mean solar time (clock time). William Molyneux printed Flamsteed's equation of time table in his book *Sciothericum Telescopicum*, published in Dublin in 1686, in which he sought to make improvements to the sundial. Early in the eighteenth

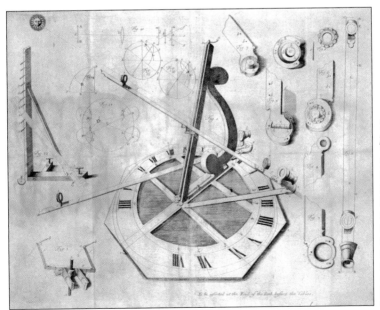

The engraved plate from 'Sciothericum Telescopicum' illustrating William Molyneux's sundial, an invention that, albeit not an equinoctial dial, must be one of the earliest precursors of the heliochronometer.

The heliochronometer invented by Abbé Guyoux, c.1827. The heliochronometer is essentially a mechanical equinoctial mean-time sundial that incorporates a mechanism to apply the equation of time correction and may allow for the difference in longitude from a standard meridian, which will directly indicate standard clock time. In c.1763 Phillip Mathias Hahn (1739–90), the German clock- and watch-maker, devised such an instrument but the sundial invented by the French cleric Abbé Jean-Marie Victor Guyoux (1793–1869) is perhaps the simplest of all heliochronometers. It comprises a basic sighting arm, pivoted at the centre of the equinoctial hour ring, fitted with two tall perpendicular vanes, one engraved with the equation of time curve, in the form of the analemma, and the other containing an aperture at its centre, through which the sun's rays could pass to project a spot of light on to the analemma. Thus, when the spot of light was centred on the appropriate point on the curve, according to the date, a pointer on the sighting arm would indicate the correct mean time on the equinoctial hour ring.

century the first dials to include this correction appeared, and the equation of time *analemma*, or figure-of-eight correction curve, took an important place in dialling literature. Nevertheless, it was not until the nineteenth century, with the

The Pilkington & Gibbs heliochronometer, widely popular in the early twentieth century. In 1906 George J. Gibbs was granted a patent for his mechanical 'universal' equinoctial mean-time sundial, or 'heliochronometer', which was not only ingenious in its invention but was simple, accurate, efficient, robust and pleasing to the eye. Its ingenuity lay in the hidden cam, beneath the date-setting disc on the equinoctial dial plate, which allowed for the equation of time correction, when the instrument was set for the particular date. The cam adjusted a sighting vane, in which a small aperture permitted the sun's rays to be projected as a spot of light on to the centre line of a second vane, situated diametrically opposite on the dial plate, when the dial plate was turned to align the vanes with the sun. The standard time could then be read off the hour scale, against a vernier, preset to correct for longitude, on the circumference of the dial plate.

Right: *The dial plate of the Pilkington & Gibbs heliochronometer, showing the alignment of the shadow vanes with the sun. These instruments were exported throughout the world and were also made in other countries under licence. It was only with the advent of modern radio communications that the sundial ceased to serve as a practical means of determining the time.*

The Pilkington 'Sol Horometer', patented in 1911. Following a dispute with George Gibbs, William Pilkington devised his own sundial for indicating mean time, but, although his instrument had certain similar features, it lacked the sophistication of the earlier model. The equinoctial dial plate comprised an outer movable hour ring, featuring a date scale, which could be turned to match the particular date against a second date scale on the inner fixed disc. This adjustment to the hour ring allowed for the equation of time.

advent of the railways, bringing rapid communication between cities and towns and creating an even greater need for accuracy in clocks and watches, that any marked improvements were made to the sundial. However, near the end of the nineteenth century, mean-time sundials, allowing for the equation of time correction, and showing clock time, were coming into use. Furthermore, mechanical equinoctial mean-time dials, or *heliochronometers*, were taking their place as useful accurate instruments. In France heliochronometers were used well into the twentieth century to check the times of departure of express trains. While the coming of the electronic age has eclipsed the sundial as a scientific instrument, modern mean-time dials are still to be seen and enjoyed. A modern example of this kind can be seen at the National Maritime Museum, commissioned to celebrate Queen Elizabeth II's Silver Jubilee in 1977. It is a fine sculpture in the form of two dolphins, whose tails cast a shadow on to the graduated dial plate. The gap between the shadows of the tails indicates the time to within a minute.

An example of Homan's Solar Chronometer (c.1912), a hemispherical equinoctial scaphe mean-time sundial. Made of copper or brass, painted black, it featured a brass semicircular equinoctial hour ring, on which the time was indicated by a thin metal rod gnomon, aligned in the polar axis of the instrument. To correct the reading from local apparent time to clock time, that is local mean time, the equation of time correction was incorporated into the semicircular hour ring, whereby, with the use of two lugs, a secondary semicircular date and hour scale ring could be manually moved, to slide against a fixed date scale. When the dates on both scales matched, for the day in question, the sundial would indicate the correct local mean time. W. M. Homan was in business in Glasgow from about 1910 to 1920. He seems to have been endeavouring to produce an inexpensive alternative to the sophisticated sundials of Pilkington & Gibbs.

The polar sundial in the mosque in Acre, Israel, evidently the only one of its kind and regarded as the most beautiful in the country. The polar dial is so named because the dial is inclined to the horizontal plane of the earth's surface at the angle of the latitude, which in the case of Acre is 33 degrees. Thus, the plane of the 'dial plate', that is the face of the dial, lies parallel to the earth's polar axis. The metal gnomon is perpendicular to the dial plate, lying in the plane of the meridian, on the 12 o'clock noon line, and also in the plane of the equinoctial, that is parallel to the earth's equator. The Acre dial is carved from a block of white and grey marble and was set up by Ahmed Basha el Jizhar in the year 1201 of the Hegira, which is the year AD 1786. Ahmed Basha (Pasha) 'The Cruel' ruled Acre from 1775 to 1804 on behalf of the Turkish government.

Polar and other unusual dials

The last primary class of sundial is the so called *polar* dial, which is one described on a plane passing through the poles of the celestial sphere and the east and west points of the horizon. It is an exceedingly rare dial, although it is partly manifest in the form of a memorial cross dial, which is a combination of direct-east, west and polar dials. The gnomon, in the case of the polar part of the dial, is the uppermost east or west edge of the 'vertical' cross-piece, while the hour lines are engraved on the uppermost surfaces of the 'horizontal' cross-piece.

A memorial cross sundial. It is aligned towards the sun, not away from it, and lies in the plane of the equinoctial, parallel to the earth's equator. It combines both polar dials with direct-east and west dials. The hour scales are engraved on the sides of the cross, while the edges that are perpendicular to the plane of the instrument indicate the time as their shadows are cast, in turn, on to these scales.

Right and below: *The great double-polar mean-time sundial, designed by the author, in the gardens of Wharfe Meadows by the river at Otley, in West Yorkshire. Set up in 1993 as a monument to Sam Chippindale, a pioneer in the design of covered shopping centres and a local philanthropist, the sundial indicates standard clock time as well as local apparent solar time. The detail (below) of the west or morning dial plate of the dial illustrates the means of reading the instrument. For the particular date, trace an imaginary horizontal line across the dial plate, parallel to the nearest lateral date line (blue for the winter months and red for when summer time is in force), to the point where it cuts the edge of the longitudinal shadow of the gnomon. Note the position of this point in relation to the closest gilded sinuous longitudinal hour line and follow this up or down to the hour scale, which will indicate the clock time, GMT or BST, while the edge of the shadow of the gnomon itself will indicate local apparent time.*

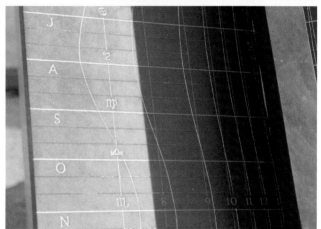

A simple but remarkable west-facing hemicylindrical equinoctial scaphe dial, cut into a tombstone in the churchyard at Saxmundham, Suffolk. There is a similar scaphe dial on the east face of the stone. The upper edge of the scaphe lies in the polar axis and acts as the gnomon.

Right: *An unusual stone monument in the form of an equinoctial sundial (or, to be more precise, a double-equinoctial sundial), resembling an anchor, set up in 1825 in the Deanery garden at Rochester, Kent. The flukes of the anchor act as the gnomons. On the shaft of the dial there is an engraved plate with a table giving the values of*

the equation of time. The enlargement of the dial block shows the edge of the fluke lying in the polar axis and its shadow indicates the time on an hour scale engraved on the shank and the stock of the anchor. In the photograph, the edge of the shadow of the fluke indicates the time to be about 11 a.m. When the shadow of the fluke is nearly in line with the edge of the stock, the time would be 12 o'clock noon.

Above: *The equiangular sundial designed by Gordon E. Taylor to mark the tercentenary of the Royal Greenwich Observatory (1676–1976), then at Herstmonceux Castle, East Sussex. The hour ring has the hours and minutes marked out in equal divisions. The gnomon is a vertical rod, slotted into the dial axis, which is moved up or down the axis on a date scale to ensure that the shadow indicates the right time.*

Right: *A modern sculptured vertical south-west declining sundial on the wall of the Marine Society's headquarters at Lambeth, London. The dial combines the symbols of the Nautical Institute (which shares the building), a symbolic armillary dial, and the Marine Society, a 'sea-dog'. The dial shows both standard and summer time. It was designed and delineated by the author, sculpted by Edwin Russell, made by Brookbrae Ltd of London, and unveiled by Her Majesty the Queen in 1979.*

The unique 'Nelson' sundial at Chatham, Kent, designed by the author and made by Ollerton Engineering of Preston. The tip of the gnomon's shadow tracks the declination arc of the anniversary of the Battle of Trafalgar on 21st October, marking the moment of Nelson's death shortly before sunset. In the photograph, the dial indicates the time to be about 11.20 a.m. on this memorable date.

Right: *A modern memorial scaphe sundial, designed by the author and executed by Mark Frith, in Plumstead cemetery, south-east London. The dial is cut as a prism, with two elements, one proclining and the other reclining. The east edge of the prism indicates the time in the morning and the west edge does so in the afternoon, casting a triangular shadow. The photograph shows the dial indicating the time as being about 8.15 a.m.*

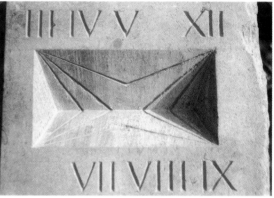

While all dials have their mathematical origin in the celestial sphere, there are some that stand out as being unusual or in a class of their own. Nevertheless, they can usually be placed without too much difficulty in one of the classes described.

A curious early-nineteenth-century 'great' declining sundial on the wall of a cottage at Seaton Ross, East Yorkshire. The gnomon is made of wood and resembles a giant paddle. The dial is attributed to William Watson (1784–1857), a local farmer, land surveyor, map-maker and amateur astronomer, with a keen interest in sundials. It is said that one of his labourers occupied the cottage and that he was often late for work, claiming that he had no clock. Watson remedied the problem by constructing the sundial.

Right: *A modern 'sundial' by the ferry at Gosport, Hampshire. Originally it was intended to be a stainless-steel flagpole at the centre of a mosaic clock-face, but the author was invited to design a means of making it work as a sundial. This was done by incorporating a nodus, which allows the sun's rays to pass through a double cone, to project a spot of light on to a noon line, when the sun is on the meridian, with corrections to give the time of 12 o'clock GMT or 1 p.m. BST. The shadow of the flagpole with its nodus can be seen in the photograph, taken at about 8 a.m., to the right of the picture on the inner edge of the blue mosaic ring. The viewer is looking south and the meridian line with its corrections is visible in the foreground in the lower half of the photograph.*

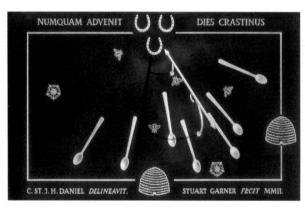

Right: *A modern shallow scaphe sundial, designed by Sir Mark Lennox-Boyd and made by Burlington Slate Ltd in 1992, sited in the wild-flower meadows in the grounds of Holker Hall, Cumbria. Measuring 5 feet 1 inch (155 cm) in diameter, with a depth of 15 inches (38 cm), the dial was conceived as a modification of the hemispherical scaphe dial or hemisphaerium of Berosus Chaldaeus, the Babylonian astronomer who is said to have flourished on the Greek island of Cos c.270 BC. Made from a flawless block from the Burlington Slate Quarry and weighing almost a tonne, the polished blue-grey dish is engraved with an hour scale, calibrated to fifteen-minute intervals, and with seven declination lines, marking the six divisions for the twelve zodiacal signs, highlighted in gold leaf. The dial is a superb example of a modern work of scientific art, relating the past to the present.*

Left: *A modern symbolic vertical declining sundial, on the wall of a barn at Cottenham, Cambridgeshire. It was designed by the author and executed in black Welsh slate by Stuart Garner in 2002. The motif of three gilded horseshoes represents the place for which the dial was made. The principal hour lines of 12 o'clock noon and 6 p.m. are each denoted by a gilded beehive, with a bee flying out along the noon line and another flying in along the 6 p.m. line towards the hive, while the hours of 9 a.m. and 3 p.m. are similarly marked out by a gilded heraldic rose with a bee flying directly along the line of the hour towards the rose. The other hour lines are marked out by seven silver gilded spoons.*

Further reading

A number of popular late-nineteenth-century and early-twentieth-century books and articles on sundials include a page or two on how to construct a sundial. To keep the instructions simple, the authors seldom explained the mathematical principles on which the art of dialling is based. There are, however, a number of good books concerned solely with the construction of sundials, some of which are included in the following list.

Brookes, A., and Stanier, M. *Cambridge Sundials*. Privately published by M. Stanier, first edition 1999.
Drinkwater, Peter I. *The Art of Sundial Construction*. Drinkwater, Shipston-on-Stour, fourth edition, 1996.
Folkard, M., and Ward, J. *Sundials Australia*. Sundials Australia, Kensington Park, South Australia, second edition 1996.
Martin, Carolyn. *A Celebration of Cornish Sundials*. Dyllansow, Truran, Redruth, 1994.
Mayall, R., and Mayall, M. *Sundials: How to Know, Use and Make Them*. Sky Publishing Corporation, Cambridge, Massachusetts, USA, 1973.
Rohr, René R. J. *Sundials – History, Theory and Practice*. University of Toronto Press, 1970.
Somerville, Andrew R. *The Ancient Sundials of Scotland*. Rogers Turner Books, London, 1990.
Stanier, Margaret. *Oxford Sundials*. Privately published by M. Stanier, second edition 2003.
Waugh, Albert E. *Sundials: Their Theory and Construction*. Dover Publications, 1973.
The *Bulletin* of the British Sundial Society.
Clocks, the International Magazine for Horological Collectors and Restorers: the sundial page (monthly).

Specialist sundial booksellers
Rogers Turner Books, 23a Nelson Road, London SE10 9JB, and 24 Rue du Buisson Richard, 78600 Le Mesnil-le-Roi, France. Telephone: 020 8853 5271.
Rita Shenton, 142 Percy Road, Twickenham, Middlesex TW2 6JG. Telephone: 020 8894 6888. Website: www.shentonbooks.com

---

Sundial makers

Brookbrae Ltd, 7 Cranleigh Gardens, Kingston-upon-Thames, Surrey KT2 5TX. Telephone: 020 8546 2110. Website: www.brookbrae.com A long-established firm in the business, specialising in large sculptured sundials.
Flowton Dials, Orchard View, Tye Lane, Flowton, Ipswich, Suffolk IP8 4LD. Telephone: 01473 658646. Website: www.btinternet.com/~johndavis Specialists in precision sundials and in the reproduction of complex historic instruments.
Lindisfarne Sundials, 43 Windsor Gardens, Bedlington, Northumberland NE22 5SY. Telephone/fax: 01670 823232. Website: www.lindisun.demon.co.uk Specialists in fine metalwork sundials and other instruments to very high standards.

The makers listed here are known to the author for the quality of their work, but there are many others who equally deserve recognition for their standards of excellence. A general list of sundial makers is available from the British Sundial Society and may also be obtained on the internet.

The remarkable facet-headed multiple sundial at Glamis Castle, Angus, with eighty component dials, believed to date from c.1670.

The British Sundial Society

Perhaps surprisingly, interest in sundials has increased greatly in recent years, particularly in Europe, where there are some very active societies, notably in Austria, France, Germany, Hungary, Italy, the Netherlands, Portugal and Spain. There are also kindred societies in North America and in Australia. The British Sundial Society was formed in 1989. Its objects are: to promote the science of gnomonics and the knowledge of all types of sundial; to catalogue the dials that still exist in the British Isles and research their history; to advise on the preservation and restoration of old sundials and the construction of new ones; to publish and circulate to members periodically a bulletin containing original articles, reports from other societies, news and other items of interest to members.

The society is intended for anyone interested in any aspect of sundials and caters not only for the expert but also for the new member seeking to learn about the subject. For further information contact:

The British Sundial Society, 4 New Wokingham Road, Crowthorne, Berkshire RG45 7NR. Telephone: 01344 772303. Website: www.sundialsoc.org.uk

---

Places to visit

Sundials can be seen in many places. The following list consists mainly of places where more than one sundial can be seen and of museums where there are sundial collections. The gardens of many other historic houses and National Trust properties contain interesting dials. Visitors are advised to check the times of opening before making a special journey.

Buckland Abbey (National Trust), Yelverton, Devon PL20 6EY. Telephone: 01822 853607. Website: www.nationaltrust.org.uk

Carnfunnock Country Park (The Time Garden), Coast Road, Ballygally, Larne, County Antrim, Northern Ireland BT40 2QG. Telephone: 028 2827 0541 or 028 2826 0088. Website: www.larne.gov.uk/carnfunnock.html

Drummond Castle Gardens, Muthill, Crieff, Perthshire PH7 4HZ. Telephone: 01764 681257. Website: www.drummondcastlegardens.co.uk

Greenwich Park, Greenwich, London SE10. Telephone: 020 8858 2608. Website: www.royalparks.gov.uk

Hever Castle, near Edenbridge, Kent TN8 7NG. Telephone: 01732 865224. Website: www.hevercastle.co.uk

Holker Hall, Cark-in-Cartmel, Grange-over-Sands, South Lakeland, Cumbria LA11 7PL. Telephone: 01539 558328. Website: www.holker-hall.co.uk The largest slate sundial in the world.

Horniman Museum, 100 London Road, Forest Hill, London SE23 3PQ. Telephone: 020 8699 1872. Website: www.horniman.ac.uk Sundial trail: it is advisable to check that sundials will be on view before visiting.

Merchant Adventurers' Hall, Fossgate, York YO1 9XD. Telephone: 01904 654818. Website: www.theyorkcompany.co.uk

Museum of the History of Science, Broad Street, Oxford OX1 3AZ. Telephone: 01865 277280. Website: www.mhs.ox.ac.uk Check before visiting that sundials will be on show.

National Maritime Museum (including the Royal Observatory), Park Road, Greenwich, London SE10 9NF. Telephone: 020 8858 4422. Website: www.nmm.ac.uk

National Memorial Arboretum, Croxall Road, Alrewas, Burton-on-Trent, Staffordshire DE13 7AR. Telephone: 01283 792333.

Penshurst Place and Gardens, Penshurst, near Tonbridge, Kent TN11 8DG. Telephone: 01892 870307. Website: www.penshurstplace.com

Royal Museum of Scotland, Chambers Street, Edinburgh EH1 1JF. Telephone: 0131 247 4219. Website: www.nms.ac.uk

Science Museum, Exhibition Road, South Kensington, London SW7 2DD. Telephone: 0870 870 4868. Website: www.sciencemuseum.org.uk

Whipple Museum of the History of Science, Department of History and Philosophy of Science, Free School Lane, Cambridge CB2 3RH. Telephone: 01223 330906. Website: www.hps.cam.ac.uk/whipple

56

Index